S0-DYE-199

A NEW VISION

What if we lived in a world where disabilities become possibilities?

By Don Lavin

First Edition
Published by
Rise, Incorporated
8406 Sunset Road NE
Spring Lake Park, Minnesota 55432 USA

This publication was produced in part through funding from the U.S. Department of Labor, Office on Disability Employment
Policy, grant award E-9-4-1-0076, and in cooperation with the Anoka County Workforce Center and its community partners.
For more information about the Anoka County Workforce Center, visit their web site at www.mnworkforcecenter.org/anoka.

Library of Congress Cataloging-in-Publication Data
          Lavin, Don
          A New Vision: What if we lived in a world where disabilities become possibilities?
          Professional
          Don Lavin — 1st ed. p. cm.
          ISBN 0-9677276-4-2
          Printed in China

Most Americans don't realize that people who have disabilities are the single largest minority population in the United States. The United States Bureau of Census and Statistics reports that 54 million people are living with some level of disability in our country. Even more amazing, the United Nations now estimates there are one-half billion people with disabilities throughout the world!

The personal, social, and economic impacts of living with a disability are often staggering. Many research studies have closely examined quality of life factors for people with disabilities in comparison to their American peers. Virtually all studies validate the existence of wide gaps in almost every important quality of life measure. For example, people with significant disabilities are far more likely to be living in poverty. They are much more likely to be unemployed, underemployed, or homeless. And people with significant disabilities are more likely to have difficulties accessing a quality education, affordable housing, adequate health care, child care, recreation and leisure, and public transportation.

As a general rule, disability is a key factor in poverty and dependency on others. In other parts of the world, children and adults with disabilities do not enjoy the same quality of life benefits as their peers. Here in the United States, most people with significant disabilities are financially dependent on some form of government assistance or welfare for a majority of their lives.

To illustrate this point, a recent Louis Harris/National Organization of Disability (NOD) Poll reports that 34 percent of adults with disabilities live in households earning less that $15,000 as compared to 12 percent of people without disabilities. Also, only 32 percent of people with significant disabilities between the ages of 18 and 64 are employed in contrast to 81 percent of all Americans. Further, people with disabilities who have jobs are more likely to report job dissatisfaction and underemployment in low paying jobs than other Americans. (Louis Harris/NOD Poll, 2001). This wide disparity between the *Haves* and the *Have-Nots* is significant and unacceptable to most fair-minded people. And what a waste of human potential!

As a society of diverse people, Americans need to accelerate the idea that social and economic justice is possible. The inclusion of all people with disabilities into every aspect of community living such as education, employment, housing, leisure and recreation and civic participation is within the reach of most people with disabilities. The scope and dimensions of this task demand improvements in a number of public policies. And more importantly, in public attitudes. Social and economic change is possible if we are willing to move ahead and share a new vision.

What if we lived in a world where disabilities become possibilities?

Don Lavin
Minneapolis, Minnesota
October, 2002

Imagine a world without disability,

where human differences aren't measured as flaws

and people are accepted for who they are.

Just belonging can open closed doors.

Imagine a world without barriers,

where anyone can go anywhere and freedom of movement is valued.

Mobility is never blocked by a stair.

Imagine the right to make choices

about where you desire to live and to rely on your own abilities.

Not the services caretakers give.

Imagine that learning is easy,

educational possibilities abound

because schools offer customized teaching.

Preferred learning styles of students are found.

Imagine having personal freedom

to become who you wanted to be,

moving forward to realize your potential.

Self-determination?

Definitely!

Orange •
Gold •
Canary •

Imagine a global economy

where EVERYONE has meaningful roles

and all job skills and talents are blended.

No more poverty, no welfare doles.

Imagine if communities of people

planned for the inclusion of all,

with increased access to public transportation,

to housing and shopping at the mall.

Imagine if we stopped labeling people,

so everyone is treated the same.

No more special places to go.

No more shame, segregation or blame.

Imagine if community-held values

were to elevate, never negate,

removing all roadblocks and obstacles

with actions to accommodate.

Imagine new paths to opportunity,

extending privilege to more than a few,

brand new policies, emerging technologies.

Creative services and family supports, too.

Imagine if circles of people,

offered friendship and helpful support

to nurture and assist one another.

A kind of caring that cannot be bought.

Imagine that it's not about money,

since every dollar in this world cannot buy

changed perceptions or increased expectations

of a naysayer unwilling to try.

Imagine that NO becomes MAYBE

and MAYBE gives way to WHY NOT!

Add hope to fuel dreams, goals and outcomes

of a people that time once forgot.

Imagine a world without disability.

Make the effort and doubtless you'll find

disability does NOT mean inability.

Only a condition conditioned by mind.

Artwork from Getty Images – Laura DeSantis, Artist
Book design – Rae Ann Wilcox